32
Warm Weather Dishes

by Helen Feingold

BARRON'S
Woodbury, New York • Toronto • London • Sydney

All inquiries should be addressed to:

Barron's Educational Series, Inc.
113 Crossways Park Drive
Woodbury, New York 11797

International Standard Book
No. 0-8120-5531-4

Library of Congress Catalog Card
No. 83-2689

**Library of Congress Cataloging in
Publication Data**
Feingold, Helen.
  32 warm-weather meals.

  (Barron's easy cooking series)
  Includes index.
  I. Cookery.   2. Cookery (Cold dishes)
I. Title.   II. Title: Thirty-two warm-weather
meals.   III. Series.
TX829.F44   1983   641.5′64   83-2689
ISBN 0-8120-5531-4

PRINTED IN THE
UNITED STATES OF AMERICA
3 4 5 6   RAE   9 8 7 6 5 4 3 2 1

Credits

Photography
Color photographs: Matthew Klein
Food preparation: Helen Feingold
Stylist: Linda Cheverton
Sources for props: Porcelain dinnerware by
    Haviland Limoges, 11 East 26 Street, N.Y. Ercuis
    Silver flatware by Ercuis at Baccarat, 55 East 57
    Street, N.Y. Crystal by Baccarat, 55 East 57
    Street, N.Y. Flowers by Howe Floral, 171 West
    23 Street, N.Y.

Food consultant Helen Feingold is a well-known
    food consultant with over 30 years experience
    in the many facets of recipe development and
    food preparation.

Cover and book design Milton Glaser, Inc.

Series editor Carole Berglie

INTRODUCTION

When the mercury starts to inch upward, the last thing you want to do is light the oven. On those hot and sticky days of summer, your family will want only a light meal—one that's cool, refreshing, and simple. And since appetites tend to wane when the temperature rises, the foods you serve need to be visually appealing as well. What better chance to practice your artistry than by arranging crisp dark spinach leaves round a salad of cubed chicken and whole shrimp (p. 7). Or crumble a hard-cooked egg yolk and sieve it onto a chilled trout in an egg and mustard sauce (p. 13). Scoop out the seeds from cucumbers and fill these light green boats with a sturdy herring salad (p. 23). If it's sandwiches instead, wow them with heros brimming over with rolled cold cuts, lettuce, tomatoes, and cucumbers.

Pretty foods don't have to be difficult or expensive, either. An easy tuna ring molded with tomato juice and gelatin is a tasty nest for a macaroni salad crunchy with carrots, peppers, and pineapple (p. 15). The loaf of smoked ham, spicy with mustard and cloves, is drizzled with a tart mustardy mayonnaise and served with a contrasting salad of sweet potatoes and fruit (p. 49). An unusual frozen salad of applesauce and raspberries is an easy freezer preparation to accompany an oven-crisped chicken served cold (p. 25).

Generally hot-weather cooking is light and simple. The favorite foods for this time of year include chicken, fish and shellfish, and salads because these foods are easy to digest, with uncomplicated flavors that are excellent served chilled. Lightness is also the key for accompaniments—crusty French breads, dry and fruity wines, fresh vegetables only just plucked from the garden. It's a time when almost everything good is in season, so you can proudly assemble the vegetable or fruit salads that are never quite as good the rest of the year. Cantaloupes have been kissed by the sun; stuff them with a zesty mix of apples, grapefruits, and melon balls (p. 9) and serve with rolls of ham filled with cream cheese. Squash vines have zucchini on them every day in summer; pick them when they are young, and blend them with eggplant, onions, mushrooms, and tomatoes for a cold ratatouille salad (p. 11).

Entertaining guests during the warm-weather months can be trying, especially if you attempt too much. Keep your menus simple and feature seemingly elegant preparations like a molded salmon mousse (p. 31) or slices of roast veal with a cauliflower sauced à la russe. For special occasions, stuff a lobster on an Italian theme. When friends are due for a luncheon, have ready the frosted loaf with its surprise of three different fillings, and decorate the platter with delicate radish flowers (p. 39). For drinks before dinner, serve the pâté (p. 41), an easy but tasty spread to accompany fresh vegetables slivered or cut in fancy shapes. Other party ideas include making miniature versions of the Meat Turnovers (p. 51) or the stuffed shrimp served with the Papaya Tropicale (p. 61).

Summer food doesn't always have to be cold; there are dishes that everyone will enjoy but that will require you to spend only a little time in the kitchen. One of these is the Speedy Taco, a Mexican-inspired mixture of beans, onions, peppers, and cheese sauce served on corn chips (p. 57). Whatever recipe you choose, remember that people generally prefer to eat less in hot weather. With these 32 recipes in hand, you'll please your family, your friends, and yourself—honest, delicious recipes for a summertime when the livin' is easy.   C.B.

BEAT THE HEAT

The key to summertime cooking is thinking ahead. If you have a full-time job, then you can prepare these foods the evening before, when the temperatures are lower. If you are at home during the day, fix your dishes in the cool of the morning. A meal that chills all day in the refrigerator is welcome after a long, steamy summer's day.

When you select your recipe, gather the ingredients and do the necessary chopping, sautéeing, or baking when it is cool. Assemble the prepared foods and wrap them to chill until the following day. Some foods are best combined and allowed to chill after blending; the flavors merge as the dish sits. Other times the components are chilled separately, to be combined immediately prior to serving for a fresh, just-prepared effect. Follow the recipes for the best results, but note that the chilling times given for each are only minimums; overnight or all day chilling work equally well.

SEASONAL SHOPPING

Starting in late spring, the markets are bursting with crisp greens and early vegetables. By summer, most vegetables reach their peak of perfection. The spring vegetables such as tiny peas, tender spinach, and delicate asparagus may be fading but in their place are dark green zucchini, *real* tomatoes, crunchy unwaxed cucumbers, slim green beans, shiny slender eggplants, plump peppers, and marvelous sweet corn. These summer vegetables are high in flavor and require only the barest of cooking. Steam them gently to retain both their taste and their nutrients.

Summer is the peak time also for fresh herbs. Now you can sprinkle fresh tarragon on your salad, mince fragrant basil over your tomatoes, snip sprigs of dill on your fish. Look for and use also the marjoram, oregano, sage, savory, and thyme that come along at this time. Even if you have a year-round windowsill garden, the outdoor herbs of summer are somehow more pungent, more flavorful.

Some fruits reach their peak in the spring or fall, but summer is a good time to buy apricots, blueberries, strawberries, cherries, peaches, plums, and, of course, melons. Increasingly, fruits are being included in main dishes rather than relegated to the end of the meal. But whether you serve them at the conclusion or use them to accent your main course, make sure the fruit you serve is perfect—totally fresh and free of blemishes.

SUMMERTIME SHORTCUTS

No one wants to spend hours in the kitchen, especially when the days are long and there are activities outside to enjoy. For the best in summertime eating without the fuss, keep your menus simple: a light entrée and a salad, perhaps with some French bread; or a cold soup, slices of meats or chicken, and a fruit salad for dessert. Concentrate your efforts on a single entrée and supplement the meal with easy side dishes that require no lengthy preparation.

Nowadays food stores often offer delicious takeaway foods of high quality and intriguing variety. Use these convenience foods to round out your meal—perhaps a take-home pasta salad to accompany a tossed green salad; or slices of country pâté to enjoy with a cold cucumber soup and French bread. Delicatessen salads are good partners with cold sliced meats, while pastry shop croissants go well with your own salads of cooked vegetables, rice and shellfish, or molded salmon mousse.

Keep jars of top-quality prepared foods on hand for sudden hot spells—herring, sardines, tuna, smoked oysters, deviled ham, pickled vegetables—plus hard-cooked eggs, bacon strips, capers, mustards, olives, and boxes of different kinds of pasta. In your freezer store extra loaves of crusty French bread and pita breads, slices of cooked chicken or turkey, prebaked pie crusts, and extra fruit sauces or purées.

When the weather cools off for a few days, take that opportunity to stock up on things you can use later when the going gets hot: roast a chicken, then freeze the meat in portions; bake muffins or a zucchini bread to accompany a meal a few days hence; barbecue a london broil which you can slice and serve cold the next day.

PARTY PLATTERS

Although the recipes in this book mostly serve 4 to 8 persons, the dishes can often be doubled or tripled and included on a seasonal buffet table when company's coming. Cold dishes work especially well because you don't have to get involved trying to keep foods hot. The dishes look good, particularly when decorated with the greens and flowers of the season, and the flavors won't fade before the food gets eaten by your guests. Now that people's tastes have shifted to the lighter side, these summer foods focus on chicken, fish, vegetables, pasta, and other favorites of the diet- or health-conscious. Select a variety of foods, make them in quantity, and arrange them attractively on your table. You can prepare everything a day or two ahead, and then spend your time enjoying your guests.

PICNICS

When the days are sunny and the breezes balmy, you and your friends would prefer to be outdoors. Picnics can be fun, especially when you don't resort to pedestrian sandwiches or boring hotdogs. Many of the recipes in this book will work well when packaged up and taken along with you. Wrap your foods carefully and include some wine, breads, cheese, fruit, and cookies in your hamper. If you are toting perishable items, however, be sure you have adequate means of keeping foods cold until they are eaten.

YIELD
6 servings

PREPARATION
15 minutes

CHILLING
1 hour

INGREDIENTS

3 cups diced cooked chicken or turkey
1 pound shrimp, cooked, shelled, and
   deveined
3 cups cooked rice
1 cup chopped celery
1/2 cup sliced stuffed olives
3 ripe tomatoes, diced
1 green pepper, diced
Mayonnaise, about 1 cup
Juice of 1 lemon
Romaine lettuce leaves
2 hard-cooked eggs, chopped

In a large bowl, mix chicken, shrimp, rice, celery, olives, tomatoes, and pepper with enough mayonnaise to make a moist mixture ①. Stir in lemon juice. Chill.

When ready to serve, line a salad bowl with lettuce leaves ②. Add salad and top with eggs. Serve with cornbread squares spread with scallion butter.

NOTE Technique photo ③ shows an easy way to chop hard-cooked eggs or egg slices by cutting them first across their width, then reinserting into the slicer and cutting them lengthwise.

YIELD
4 servings

PREPARATION
30 minutes

CHILLING
30 minutes

INGREDIENTS
8 slices boiled ham
1 package (8 ounces) cream cheese
2 tablespoons milk
2 tablespoons minced celery
2 sweet gherkins, minced
2 small cantaloupes
2 grapefruit, peeled and cut into
   sections
2 red apples, cored and diced
1 cup prepared French dressing

2 tablespoons honey
2 tablespoons lemon juice
Strawberries and kiwifruit slices

2

Spread ham slices with a mixture of cream cheese, milk, celery, and gherkins ①. Roll up slices starting at the narrow end ②. Wrap and chill.

Halve the cantaloupes and remove seeds. Cut a thin slice from bottom of each half to allow it to stand straight. Cut melon balls from cantaloupe ③.

Mix melon balls, grapefruit sections, and apples in a bowl. Beat dressing with honey and lemon juice, then pour over fruit.

Scrape out melon shells and drain off excess liquid. Fill with fruit mixture and place on serving plates. Cut ham rolls into ½-inch-thick slices and place around melons. Garnish with hulled strawberries and kiwi slices, and serve with blueberry muffins.

LONDON BROIL WITH RATATOUILLE SALAD

YIELD
6 servings

PREPARATION
15 minutes

COOKING
50 minutes

CHILLING
1–2 hours

INGREDIENTS

1 london broil, about 3 pounds
1 clove garlic, crushed
2 teaspoons cracked pepper
2 tablespoons olive oil
1 cup garlic-flavored vinaigrette
1 green pepper
1 large onion
2 garlic cloves
1 large eggplant
2 zucchini

½ pound mushrooms
1 can (1 pound) tomatoes with juice
Salt and pepper

Spread london broil with garlic, pepper, and oil ①. Broil for 10 minutes on each side for rare, 12 minutes for medium. Cool and then chill.

Chop the green pepper, slice the onion, and mince the garlic. Leave skin on eggplant, but cut away stem and chop into medium dice ②. Slice the zucchini and wipe the mushrooms clean with a damp towel and then slice.

Place vinaigrette dressing into a large saucepan. Add chopped vegetables and tomatoes with the juice. Simmer uncovered until vegetables are soft and mushy, about 30 minutes. Season to taste with salt and pepper. Cool and then chill.

When ready to serve, cut london broil into thin slices ③ and serve with ratatouille salad. Have crusty rolls and chive butter alongside.

CHILLED TROUT WITH EGG AND MUSTARD SAUCE

YIELD
6 servings

PREPARATION
15 minutes

COOKING
30 minutes

CHILLING
1–2 hours

INGREDIENTS

6 fresh or frozen trout
1 cup chicken broth
Juice of 1 lemon
½ teaspoon salt
2 hard-cooked eggs, finely chopped
2 tablespoons finely chopped parsley
2 tablespoons finely chopped scallions
1 cup plain yogurt
½ cup mayonnaise
1 tablespoon prepared mustard

Preheat oven to 350 degrees. Place trout side by side in a shallow baking dish. Add chicken broth, lemon juice, and salt ①. Cover with foil ② and bake in moderate oven for 30 minutes. Remove from oven and cool covered. Chill for several hours.

In a bowl, combine remaining ingredients and stir until well blended. Season to taste with salt.

Remove trout from cooking liquid and drain on paper towels. Strip off skin ③ and remove heads and tails.

Place trout on serving platter and spoon sauce evenly over them. Chill until ready to serve. Garnish with fresh parsley, dill, lemon slices and, if desired, sieved hard-cooked egg yolks. Serve with puff pastry strips.

NOTE Puff pastry is available in the freezer section of most supermarkets.

YIELD
4–6 servings

PREPARATION
15 minutes

CHILLING
2–3 hours

RING
2 envelopes unflavored gelatin
3½ cups tomato juice
Juice of 1 lemon
1 tablespoon Worcestershire sauce
1 small onion, grated
2 cans (7 ounces each) tuna, drained
   and flaked
1 cup minced celery

MACARONI SALAD
3 cups cooked elbow macaroni
1 cup shredded carrots
1 green pepper, chopped
1 can (1 pound, 4 ounces) pineapple
   chunks, drained
⅓ cup mayonnaise
⅓ cup sour cream

Mix gelatin and ½ cup of the juice in a small saucepan. Stir over low heat until mixture is hot. Pour into a bowl and stir in remaining tomato juice, lemon juice, and Worcestershire sauce. Chill until slightly thickened and syrupy.

Fold onion, tuna, and celery into gelatin mixture. Pour mixture into a lightly oiled 6-cup ring mold. Chill until firm.

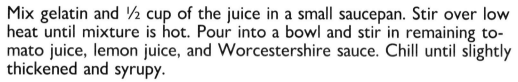

For salad, mix macaroni with carrots, pepper, pineapple chunks, and mayonnaise and sour cream. Chill.

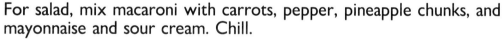

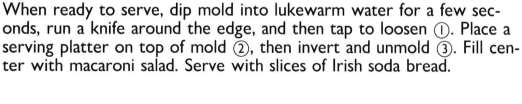

When ready to serve, dip mold into lukewarm water for a few seconds, run a knife around the edge, and then tap to loosen ①. Place a serving platter on top of mold ②, then invert and unmold ③. Fill center with macaroni salad. Serve with slices of Irish soda bread.

YIELD
6 servings

PREPARATION
20 minutes

BAKING
45 minutes

CHILLING
1–2 hours

MEATLOAF
1 pound ground chuck
1 egg
1 teaspoon salt
1/4 teaspoon pepper
1 cup herb stuffing mix
1/2 cup tomato juice
1 small onion, chopped

TOPPING
1/2 cup catsup
1/4 cup well-drained pickle relish
1 tablespoon prepared mustard

SANDWICHES
12 slices rye bread
6 slices pumpernickel bread
12 thin slices red onion
12 strips crisp bacon
Lettuce leaves

6

Preheat the oven to 350 degrees. Combine the meatloaf ingredients in a bowl and mix until well blended ①. Shape mixture into a long narrow loaf on a foil-lined shallow baking pan ②. Bake in a moderate oven for 40 to 45 minutes. Cool, wrap, and chill.

Mix catsup, relish, and mustard. Chill.

When ready to serve, spread 6 of the rye slices and all the pumpernickel slices with catsup mixture ③. Cut meatloaf into thin slices and place 6 of the rye slices on serving plates. Top with meatloaf slices and red onion slices. Add pumpernickel slices, more meatloaf slices, and bacon strips. Add lettuce leaves. Top with plain rye slices.

If desired, cut sandwiches in half and spear each half with a toothpick. Serve with rippled potato chips, a tossed green salad, or pickled mixed vegetables.

SCALLOPS AND MUSSELS REMOULADE

YIELD
6 servings

PREPARATION
25 minutes

COOKING
20 minutes

CHILLING
1–2 hours

INGREDIENTS

48 mussels
1 pound sea scallops
1 small onion, chopped
1 clove garlic, chopped
1 cup dry white wine
1 cup chicken broth
1 cup mayonnaise
Juice of 1 lime
1 dill pickle, minced
1 tablespoon prepared mustard

1 tablespoon finely chopped parsley
1 tablespoon finely chopped chives
Boston lettuce leaves

Scrub mussels and pull off the beards—those black stringy sections ①. Place mussels and scallops into a large saucepan. Add onion, garlic, wine, and chicken broth ②. Cover and simmer gently for 15 to 20 minutes or until mussel shells open. Drain and cool. (Broth may be used chilled as a flavorful first course, topped with lime slices.)

Remove mussels from shells ③ and place into a bowl along with scallops. Mix remaining ingredients except lettuce leaves and add to seafood. Blend thoroughly, then chill.

Serve spooned onto lettuce leaves. If desired, sprinkle with paprika, additional parsley, or chives. Serve with marinated asparagus spears and sliced tomatoes.

YIELD
6 servings

PREPARATION
20 minutes

COOKING
25 minutes

CHILLING
2–3 hours

INGREDIENTS
6 chicken cutlets, about 2 pounds
Salt and pepper
Flour for dusting
1/3 cup butter or margarine
1 can (6 1/2 ounces) tuna, drained
2 cloves garlic
2 tablespoons anchovy paste
1/2 cup olive oil
1/4 cup red wine vinegar
1/4 cup heavy cream
Chopped parsley
Drained capers

8

Sprinkle chicken cutlets with salt and pepper. Dip chicken into flour and coat ①. Shake off all excess flour.

Heat butter in a large skillet and brown chicken breasts slowly until they are cooked, about 25 minutes. Remove from pan, drain on absorbent paper ②, and place on a serving platter. Cover and chill.

Place remaining ingredients except parsley and capers into a blender ③ and whirl until smooth. Pour sauce evenly over chicken and chill several hours.

Serve chicken sprinkled with parsley and capers, and accompanied by marinated tomato slices, artichoke hearts, and black olives.

YIELD
6 servings

PREPARATION
30 minutes

CHILLING
1–3 hours

INGREDIENTS
6 large cucumbers
1 jar (12 ounces) herring tidbits in
   wine sauce
3 potatoes, cooked, peeled, and diced
2 beets, cooked and shredded
½ cup chopped celery
1 dill pickle, chopped
1 tart apple, peeled, cored, and diced
2 tablespoons chopped fresh dill
½ cup heavy cream, whipped
Salt
Bibb lettuce leaves

Cut cucumbers in half lengthwise, and with a spoon scrape out the seeds ① and discard them. Carefully peel the cucumbers ②, wrap in plastic, and chill.

Drain the herring and chop. Mix with potatoes, beets, celery, pickle, apple, and dill in a large bowl ③. Fold in cream and season to taste with salt, if necessary. Chill.

When ready to serve, cut a thin slice from bottom of each cucumber half to allow it to stand upright. Place cucumbers on serving plates, and fill with herring mixture. Present on a platter lined with lettuce leaves and, if desired, serve with flat bread and paper-thin slices of Danish cheese.

YIELD
6 servings

PREPARATION
35 minutes

COOKING
45 minutes

FREEZING
4–5 hours

INGREDIENTS

6 large chicken legs
Salt and pepper
1 egg, well beaten
2 cups cornflake crumbs
½ cup grated parmesan cheese
½ teaspoon oregano
½ teaspoon garlic powder
½ cup melted butter or margarine
2 cups applesauce
½ cup orange juice
2 tablespoons lemon juice

2 egg whites
¼ cup sugar
½ cup heavy cream, whipped
1 package (10 ounces) frozen
    raspberries, thawed

Preheat the oven to 350 degrees. Sprinkle chicken with salt and pepper. Dip legs into egg and then into a mixture of crumbs, cheese, oregano, and garlic powder ①. Press firmly to make crumbs adhere.

Brush a shallow baking pan with some of the butter. Add the chicken legs and drizzle the remaining butter over legs. Bake in a moderate oven for 40 to 45 minutes. Cool and then chill.

In a bowl, mix applesauce with orange and lemon juices. Beat egg whites until they form soft peaks. Beat in the sugar, 1 tablespoon at a time, until eggs form stiff peaks. Fold into applesauce mixture, then fold in whipped cream ②. Pour mixture into a foil-lined 8½ × 4½ × 2½-inch loaf pan.

Purée raspberries in a blender and press through a sieve. Spoon purée over applesauce mixture, then, with a knife, swirl the raspberry into the applesauce mixture ③. Place in freezer and freeze until hard, about 4 hours.

When ready to serve, pull salad out of pan using foil, strip off foil, and cut into slices. Serve with cold chicken and slices of banana bread, if desired.

YIELD
6 servings

PREPARATION
25 minutes

COOKING
15 minutes

CHILLING
2 hours

INGREDIENTS
1 pound raw shrimp
1/2 pound thin spaghetti or transparent
   noodles
2 cups diced tofu
1 cup peanut or sesame oil
1/3 cup red wine vinegar
1/2 teaspoon red pepper flakes
2 tablespoons smooth peanut butter
1/3 cup Japanese soy sauce
1 clove garlic, mashed
1/3 cup finely chopped salted peanuts
6 scallions, trimmed and sliced

Cook, shell, and devein shrimp. Wrap and chill.

Cook noodles in boiling salted water until tender, then drain and pour into a bowl ①. Add tofu and shrimp ②.

In a bowl, beat oil with vinegar, red pepper flakes, peanut butter, soy sauce, and garlic until well blended and thick ③.

Pour sauce over noodles and toss to coat all particles. Cover and chill for 1 to 2 hours. When ready to serve, toss noodles again and sprinkle with peanuts and scallions. Serve with snow peas.

YIELD
4 servings

PREPARATION
15 minutes

COOKING
1–1½ hours

CHILLING
2–3 hours

INGREDIENTS
2 pound boneless veal or pork roast
Salt and pepper
½ teaspoon thyme
6 slices bacon
1 large head cauliflower
½ cup sour cream
½ cup French dressing
Juice of 1 lemon
2 tablespoons drained capers
¼ cup minced pimiento
2 tablespoons chopped chives
Dash of garlic powder

Preheat the oven to 350 degrees. Sprinkle roast with salt, pepper, and thyme. Cover with bacon slices ①. Place in a shallow roasting pan and roast in a moderate oven for 1 hour. Cool meat, wrap, and then chill.

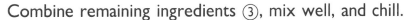

Steam cauliflower (trim head and leave it whole) over boiling salted water for 15 to 20 minutes or until easily pierced but still somewhat firm ②. Drain, cool, and chill.

Combine remaining ingredients ③, mix well, and chill.

When ready to serve, cut meat into thin slices. Place slices on serving platter along with cauliflower and top with sauce. Cut cauliflower into wedges to serve, and accompany with a salad of red peppers.

YIELD
6 to 8 servings

PREPARATION
20 minutes

CHILLING
3 hours

INGREDIENTS

2 envelopes unflavored gelatin
½ cup cold water
⅓ cup lemon juice
3 cans (7 ounces each) salmon
1 cup mayonnaise
1½ cups finely chopped celery
⅓ cup finely chopped green pepper
2 scallions, chopped
Salt and pepper
Lettuce leaves
Cucumber slices

In a saucepan, combine gelatin, cold water, and lemon juice. Stir over medium heat until mixture is very hot.

Drain, skin, bone, and then flake the salmon ①. In a bowl, mix salmon, mayonnaise, celery, green pepper, and scallions. Stir in gelatin mixture. Season to taste with salt and pepper.

Spray a 6-cup mold with Pam or lightly oil it ②. Pour gelatin mixture into mold ③ and chill until firm, about 3 hours.

To unmold, dip mold into lukewarm water for a few seconds, tap to loosen, and invert onto a platter. Garnish mousse with lettuce leaves and cucumber slices. Serve with herb biscuits and black olives.

YIELD
6 servings

PREPARATION
10 minutes

CHILLING
1 hour

INGREDIENTS
2 cups flaked crab meat
1 cup chopped celery and leaves
½ cup sliced pitted black olives
2 tablespoons chopped chives
3 hard-cooked eggs, chopped
Sour cream, about ½ cup
Salt
3 avocados, halved and seeded
Lemon juice
3 navel oranges

In a bowl, mix crab meat, celery, olives, chives, eggs, and enough sour cream to make a moist mixture ①. Season to taste with salt.

Place avocados on serving plates and sprinkle the cut surface with lemon juice to prevent darkening ②. Fill hollows with crab mixture. Peel the oranges and divide into sections ③. Surround avocados with orange sections. Chill until ready to serve. Serve with cold borscht topped with sour cream and slices of pumpernickel bread.

YIELD
4 servings

PREPARATION
10 minutes

CHILLING
30 minutes

INGREDIENTS

8 slices boiled ham
8 slices swiss cheese
8 slices turkey breast
8 slices roast beef
4 8-inch-long Italian breads
4 cups shredded lettuce
2 ripe tomatoes, sliced
1 cucumber, peeled and sliced
4 scallions, trimmed (optional)
½ cup Italian salad dressing

Distribute ham slices on work surface and top each slice with a slice of cheese, turkey, and roast beef. Roll up into 8 rolls ①. Wrap and chill.

When ready to serve, cut breads horizontally. Place bottom half of bread on serving plates. Sprinkle on lettuce. Cut rolls of meat into ½-inch-thick slices ② and place on lettuce. Top with tomatoes, cucumber slices, and scallions, if desired ③. Drizzle dressing over top. Replace top of bread. If desired, cut each bread into 4 pieces for easy eating, and serve with cold avocado soup.

ITALIAN STUFFED LOBSTER WITH ARTICHOKES

YIELD
4 servings

PREPARATION
30 minutes

COOKING
40 minutes

CHILLING
1–2 hours

INGREDIENTS

4 lobsters, each weighing 1 1/2 pounds
4 artichokes
1 cup (4 ounces) diced mozzarella
   cheese
4 plum tomatoes, diced
3 egg yolks
3 cloves garlic
1 tablespoon lemon juice
1/2 teaspoon salt
1/4 teaspoon pepper

1 cup olive oil
1/4 cup chicken broth
4 anchovy fillets
1/2 cup toasted pine nuts
8 pitted black olives, sliced

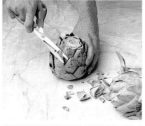

Drop lobsters into boiling salted water. When water reboils, boil for 5 minutes, then drain and cool.

Trim stems and tips of leaves on artichokes ①, and cook in boiling salted water until easily pierced, about 30 to 35 minutes. Drain, cool, and then chill.

With a sharp knife, cut lobsters in half and open out ②. Remove meat from body and claws ③. Dice meat and mix with mozzarella cheese and tomatoes. Stuff mixture back into body shells. Chill.

Combine egg yolks, garlic, lemon juice, salt, and pepper in a blender. Whirl until smooth. With motor running, slowly add oil drop by drop until all oil is added. Slowly drip in chicken broth. Add anchovy fillets and blend until smooth. Chill.

When ready to serve, thin dressing, if necessary, to a heavy cream consistency using extra chicken broth. Drizzle some of the dressing over lobster salad. Sprinkle with pine nuts and olives. Place remaining dressing into small bowls and use for dipping artichoke leaves. This is good accompanied by sesame seed breadsticks.

17

YIELD
8 to 10 servings

PREPARATION
15 minutes

CHILLING
2 hours

INGREDIENTS
2-pound loaf unsliced white bread
1 package (8 ounces) cream cheese
1/3 cup milk
Radish roses
Green pepper leaves

CHEESE FILLING
1/3 cup finely chopped pecans
1/2 cup shredded sharp cheddar cheese
1 tablespoon prepared mustard
1/3 cup mayonnaise

HAM FILLING
1 can (4 1/2 ounces) deviled ham
1/4 cup finely chopped black olives
2 tablespoons chopped pimiento
1 tablespoon chili sauce

EGG FILLING
4 hard-cooked eggs, chopped
2 tablespoons finely chopped chives
1/4 cup mayonnaise

Trim crusts from bread, leaving a long block of white bread ①. Cut bread into 4 lengthwise slices ②.

Combine each of the filling ingredients in a bowl and mix until well blended. Place 1 bread slice on serving platter and spread with cheese filling ③. Top with second bread slice and ham filling. Top with third slice and egg filling. Top with remaining bread slice.

Beat cream cheese and milk until soft and fluffy. Spread the top and sides of the loaf with cheese mixture. Chill until firm, about 2 hours.

Serve loaf garnished with radish roses and green pepper leaves. To serve, cut into thick slices with a serrated knife using a gentle sawing motion. Accompany with olives, pickles, and radishes and, if desired, a chilled consommé madrilene.

39

YIELD
6 servings

PREPARATION
20 minutes

COOKING
20–25 minutes

CHILLING
1–2 hours

INGREDIENTS
1 pound good-quality liverwurst
1 package (3 ounces) cream cheese
1/4 cup butter
1/3 cup minced pitted black olives
1 clove garlic, mashed
Assorted raw vegetables: carrots,
zucchini, mushrooms, tomatoes,
celery, broccoli or cauliflower
flowerets

FRITTATA
10 eggs
1/4 cup water
2 teaspoons salt
2 tablespoons olive oil
1 green pepper, chopped
1 onion, chopped
3 tomatoes, chopped

In a bowl, mix liverwurst with cream cheese and butter until soft and fluffy ①. Fold in olives and garlic. Place into serving bowl. Chill.

Cut the vegetables into desired pieces: slice the carrots and zucchini, remove stems from mushrooms and flute caps, cut tomatoes into wedges, chunk celery, separate broccoli or cauliflower flowerets. Wrap and chill vegetables.

When ready, prepare frittata. Beat eggs with water and salt. In a large 10-inch skillet, heat olive oil and sauté the pepper and onion for 10 minutes. Add tomatoes and sauté for another 5 minutes. Add eggs ② and cook without stirring until golden brown on the bottom. Place skillet under broiler 8 inches away from source of heat ③ and broil until egg is golden and feels firm to the touch. Remove from broiler and cool. Invert frittata onto a serving platter. Serve pâté with vegetables around it. Serve frittata cold, cut into long, thin wedges. Accompany with rye toast.

YIELD
6 servings

PREPARATION
20 minutes

COOKING
15 minutes

INGREDIENTS

3 cups cubed iceberg lettuce
3 cups torn pieces romaine
1 cup radish slices
½ cup white onion rings
4 ounces crumbled feta cheese or
    farmer cheese
3 tomatoes, cut into wedges
1 can (2 ounces) anchovy fillets,
    drained
18 black or Greek olives
1 cucumber, cut into thin slices

½ cup olive oil
¼ cup red wine vinegar
½ teaspoon salt
¼ teaspoon pepper
½ teaspoon oregano
1 teaspoon sugar
6 pita breads
1 pound mozzarella cheese, shredded

In a large bowl, mix lettuce, romaine, radishes, onion rings, feta cheese, tomatoes, anchovies, olives, and cucumber ①. Cover and chill.

In a bowl, beat oil with vinegar, salt, pepper, oregano, and sugar until thick ②. Let stand at room temperature.

Slash pita breads at one side and stuff each with mozzarella cheese ③.

When almost ready to serve, preheat oven to 400 degrees. Place pita breads into hot oven for 15 minutes. Cool 5 minutes, then cut into quarters. Meanwhile, beat dressing again and pour over salad. Toss to coat all particles. Serve pita breads warm with dressed salad.

TUNA SALAD PIE

YIELD
6 servings

PREPARATION
40 minutes

COOKING
25 minutes

CHILLING
1–2 hours

INGREDIENTS

1 envelope unflavored gelatin
1/3 cup lemon juice
1 cup mayonnaise
1/2 cup tomato juice
1 tablespoon Worcestershire sauce
1 small green pepper, chopped
1 cup chopped celery
2 cans (7 ounces each) tuna, drained
   and flaked
3 hard-cooked eggs, sliced

2 ripe tomatoes, peeled, seeded, and
   chopped

PIE CRUST

1/2 cup vegetable shortening
1 1/2 cups all-purpose flour
Dash of salt
3 tablespoons cold water,
   approximately

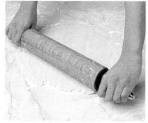

Make crust first. Place shortening and flour in a large bowl. Add salt. Cut shortening into flour and blend until mixture resembles coarse meal. Add water and stir with a fork until the dough cleans the bowl. Form into a smooth ball, wrap in wax paper, and chill 30 minutes.

Preheat oven to 400 degrees. Roll out pie crust on floured surface ①. Fold it in quarters to make it easy to transfer to pan ②. Unfold, trim edges, and crimp ③. Prick bottom of shell with a fork, line with foil, and fill with rice or beans. Bake for 20 minutes. Remove foil and bake shell for another 5 minutes or until brown. Let cool.

In a small saucepan, mix gelatin and lemon juice. Stir over low heat until gelatin is dissolved. Stir in mayonnaise, tomato juice, and Worcestershire sauce. Chill until slightly thickened.

When mixture has thickened slightly, fold in green pepper, celery, and tuna. Pour mixture into pie shell. Top with egg slices and chopped tomatoes. Chill until firm.

Cut into wedges to serve with a tossed green salad.

NOTE *You may substitute a premade, pre-cooked 9-inch pie shell or use an 11-ounce package of pie crust mix.*

YIELD
6 servings

PREPARATION
15 minutes

COOKING
20 minutes

CHILLING
1 hour

INGREDIENTS
18 large pasta shells
1½ cups finely chopped cooked
   chicken
1½ cups finely chopped cooked ham
½ cup minced celery
1 tart apple, peeled, cored, and
   chopped
2 sweet gherkins, minced
⅓ cup mayonnaise
Juice of 1 lemon
Pinch of dry mustard
Salt

COLE SLAW
3 cups shredded red cabbage
3 cups shredded green cabbage
1 small onion, minced
⅓ cup mayonnaise
⅓ cup sour cream
1 teaspoon celery seed

Cook pasta shells in boiling salted water according to package directions. Drain and place into cold water ①.

Mix chicken, ham, celery, apple, gherkins, mayonnaise, lemon juice, and mustard ②. Season to taste with salt.

Drain shells and dry on absorbent paper. Stuff shells with salad mixture ③ and place on serving platter. Spoon extra salad around shells, and chill.

Mix ingredients for cole slaw in a bowl until well blended, then chill.

Serve shells with red and white cole slaw and slices of crusty Italian bread.

YIELD
6 servings

PREPARATION
15 minutes

BAKING
1 hour

CHILLING
1–2 hours

INGREDIENTS
4 cups ground smoked ham
1/2 cup minced celery
4 slices white bread, crumbled
2 eggs
1/3 cup minced onions
1 tablespoon prepared mustard
1/4 teaspoon ground cloves
2 tablespoons frozen orange juice
   concentrate
2 tablespoons honey

SAUCE
1 egg
1 tablespoon prepared mustard
1/2 cup corn oil
1/4 cup cider vinegar
1 teaspoon salt
1 teaspoon sugar

Preheat oven to 350 degrees. In a bowl, mix ground ham, celery, bread, eggs, onions, and mustard. Press mixture into a greased loaf pan ①—an easy way to shape a loaf—then unmold onto a greased, shallow baking pan ②. Bake in a moderate oven for 40 minutes.

In a small bowl, mix cloves, orange juice concentrate, and honey. Spread mixture over ham and bake for another 15 minutes. Remove ham from oven and cool. Wrap and chill for 1–2 hours.

Combine sauce ingredients in a blender ③ and whirl until smooth. Cut loaf into slices and place on serving plates. Spoon sauce over slices and serve with a salad of sweet potatoes, pineapple chunks, and mandarin oranges. Accompany with crescent rolls.

YIELD
4 servings

PREPARATION
25 minutes

COOKING
30 minutes

CHILLING
1–2 hours

INGREDIENTS
1 package (11 ounces) pie crust mix
¼ cup butter or margarine
1 onion, chopped
1 green pepper, chopped
1 can (1 pound) corned beef hash
¼ cup catsup
1 egg, well beaten
½ cup well-drained pickle relish
   (optional)
½ cup cranberry-orange relish
   (optional)

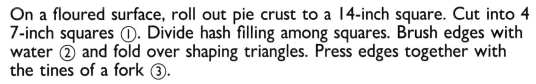

Prepare pie crust mix according to package directions. Wrap and chill for 30 minutes.

Heat butter in a skillet and sauté onion and green pepper for 5 minutes. Stir in hash and catsup. Cool.

On a floured surface, roll out pie crust to a 14-inch square. Cut into 4 7-inch squares ①. Divide hash filling among squares. Brush edges with water ② and fold over shaping triangles. Press edges together with the tines of a fork ③.

Preheat oven to 400 degrees. Place turnovers on a greased cookie sheet and brush with beaten egg. Prick the tops with a fork, then bake in hot oven for 25 to 30 minutes or until crust is richly browned. Cool.

Serve turnovers cold, topped, if desired, with pickle relish mixed with cranberry-orange relish.

DEVILED EGGS WITH PASTA SALAD

YIELD
6 servings

PREPARATION
20 minutes

CHILLING
1 hour

INGREDIENTS
9 hard-cooked eggs
2 tablespoons chopped chives
1 tablespoon prepared mustard
9 stuffed olives, minced
Mayonnaise
8 ounces spinach noodles, cooked and
    drained
4 scallions, trimmed and sliced
2 carrots, shredded
1 cup Italian salad dressing
6 plum tomatoes, thinly sliced

Cut eggs in half. Remove yolks ① and place into a bowl; reserve whites. Mash yolks ② and mix with chives, mustard, olives, and enough mayonnaise to make a thick, creamy mixture. Stuff mixture into reserved egg whites ③. Chill.

In a bowl, mix noodles, scallions, carrots, and dressing. Chill.

When ready to serve, place a portion of pasta salad on each plate and top each with 3 egg halves. Garnish with sliced tomatoes.

25

YIELD
6 servings

PREPARATION
20 minutes

COOKING
35 minutes

CHILLING
2–3 hours

INGREDIENTS

6 salmon steaks, each 1 inch thick
Salt
½ cup chicken broth
½ cup dry white wine
1 lemon, sliced
2 white grapefruits
2 pink grapefruits
2 navel oranges
¾ cup coarsely chopped brazil nuts
¼ cup lemon juice

½ cup corn oil
½ cup heavy cream
¼ cup finely chopped flaked coconut
Shredded romaine leaves

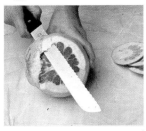

Preheat oven to 350 degrees. Sprinkle salmon with salt and place steaks into a shallow foil-lined baking pan, side by side. Add chicken broth, wine, and lemon slices ①. Cover with foil and bake in a moderate oven for 30 to 35 minutes, or until salmon is pale pink. Cool and then chill covered.

Peel the grapefruits ② and divide into sections ③. Peel and section the oranges. In a bowl, mix grapefruits, oranges, and nuts. Chill.

Beat lemon juice, oil, cream, and coconut in a bowl and chill.

When ready to serve, drain salmon and remove skin and bones. Place a salmon steak on each plate and add grapefruit and orange mixture. Beat dressing again and spoon over salmon and salad. Serve garnished with shredded romaine leaves, and accompany with onion bread.

26

YIELD
4 servings

PREPARATION
5 minutes

COOKING
20 minutes

INGREDIENTS
2 tablespoons corn oil
I green pepper, chopped
2 onions, sliced
I can (I pound) kidney beans, drained
2 cans (10½ ounces each) condensed
   cream of mushroom soup
I cup milk
2 cups (8 ounces) shredded sharp
   cheddar cheese
2 cups taco chips or corn chips
4 slices crisp bacon, crumbled

In a skillet, heat oil and sauté pepper and onions for I0 minutes or until pale golden brown. Add beans ① and heat until hot.

Combine soup, milk, and cheese ② in a saucepan and heat until cheese melts and mixture bubbles.

Place chips on individual serving plates and add sautéed beans and onions. Spoon on the cheese mixture and sprinkle with crisp bacon. Spike the mixture with green or red hot sauce and accompany with guacamole, if desired.

YIELD
6 servings

PREPARATION
10 minutes

BAKING
1 hour

CHILLING
1–2 hours

INGREDIENTS
6 Cornish game hens (thawed if
    frozen), giblets removed
Salt and pepper
1½ cups barbecue sauce
Juice of 1 lemon
½ cup burgundy wine

APPLE SALAD
3 Bibb lettuces
4 large apples
1 cup sliced celery
½ cup coarsely broken walnuts
Mayonnaise, about ¾ cup

Preheat oven to 350 degrees. Sprinkle game hens inside and out with salt and pepper. Place in foil-lined pan. Roast in a moderate oven for 1 hour.

Mix barbecue sauce, lemon juice, and wine. Brush this mixture over game hens every 10 minutes during roasting ①. When done, wrap and chill.

Peel and core apples ②, then dice. In a bowl, mix apples, celery, and walnuts. Stir in enough mayonnaise to make a moist mixture. Chill.

Serve game hens on individual plates. Cut lettuce in half ③ and add lettuce halves to plates; top with apple mixture. Serve with warmed muffins.

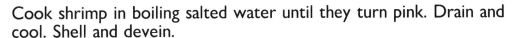

YIELD
6 servings

PREPARATION
25 minutes

COOKING
5 minutes

CHILLING
1–2 hours

INGREDIENTS

2 pounds raw shrimp
1 package (3 ounces) cream cheese
½ cup finely chopped scallions
3 papayas
½ cup sliced water chestnuts
1 can (20 ounces) pineapple chunks,
   drained
1 cup seedless green grapes
½ cup mayonnaise
½ cup pineapple juice

1 tablespoon minced crystallized
   ginger
6 tablespoons toasted slivered almonds

Cook shrimp in boiling salted water until they turn pink. Drain and cool. Shell and devein.

Slash shrimp lengthwise ① but not cutting all the way through. Stuff cut with some of the cream cheese. Dip shrimp stuffing into scallions ②. Chill.

Cut papayas into halves and remove seeds ③. Mix water chestnuts, pineapple, and grapes; spoon mixture on papayas. Chill.

When ready to serve, place papayas on serving plates and surround with stuffed shrimp.

Mix mayonnaise and pineapple juice, then fold in ginger. Spoon dressing over fruit. Serve sprinkled with almonds.

POACHED FISH FILLETS WITH DILL SAUCE

YIELD

4 servings

PREPARATION

10 minutes

COOKING

25 minutes

CHILLING

3–4 hours

INGREDIENTS

4 flounder fillets
4 scallions, minced
Salt
1 cup chicken broth
1/2 cup dry white wine
2 tablespoons chopped fresh dill
1/2 cup mayonnaise
Finely shredded lettuce leaves
Chopped fresh dill

Sprinkle flounder fillets with scallions and salt. Roll up each jelly roll fashion and place seam side down in a skillet. Add chicken broth, wine, and dill. Cover and simmer gently for 20 to 25 minutes or until fish turns white and flakes easily.

Cool fish in broth, then remove fish rolls with a slotted spoon and place on serving platter. Chill.

Boil pan juices until only 1/2 cup remains. Cool and then mix juices with mayonnaise until smooth. Spoon mixture over fish. Chill. Surround fish with shredded lettuce sprinkled with dill and serve with a saffron rice salad.

SPICED LUNCHEON MEAT WITH FRUIT SALAD

YIELD

6 servings

PREPARATION

20 minutes

COOKING

40 minutes

CHILLING

1–2 hours

INGREDIENTS

2 cans (12 ounces each) luncheon
   meat
Whole cloves
1/2 cup apricot preserves
1/2 cup firmly packed brown sugar
1 tablespoon prepared mustard
1 large pineapple, cut in half
1 can (11 ounces) mandarin oranges,
   drained

2 bananas, sliced
1 cup miniature marshmallows
1 cup flaked coconut
1 cup (1/2 pint) sour cream

Preheat oven to 350 degrees. Place luncheon meat on a shallow baking pan. Press 8 cloves into top of each loaf. Mix apricot preserves, brown sugar, and mustard. Spread mixture over top of meat. Bake in a moderate oven for 35 to 40 minutes, spooning pan juices over meat every 10 minutes. Cool and then chill.

Cut meat from pineapple and reserve shells. Dice pineapple and place into a bowl. Add remaining ingredients and stir to blend well. Spoon mixture into pineapple shells. Chill.

When ready to serve, place pineapple halves on a serving platter and surround with thin slices of luncheon meat.

CHICKEN AND NEW POTATO SALAD

31

YIELD
4 servings

PREPARATION
20 minutes

CHILLING
1–2 hours

INGREDIENTS

¾ cup mayonnaise
¼ cup chicken broth
1 teaspoon curry powder
3 tablespoons minced scallions
3 cups diced cooked chicken, turkey,
   or duckling

2 cups 1-inch pieces cooked green
   beans
8 new potatoes, cooked unpeeled and
   halved
⅓ cup chopped pecans
Salt and pepper

In a large bowl, combine all ingredients and mix until well blended, adding salt and pepper to taste. Chill. Serve with tomato slices and warm popovers.

LENTIL AND SALAMI SALAD

32

YIELD
4 to 6 servings

PREPARATION
10 minutes

COOKING
45 minutes

CHILLING
1 hour

INGREDIENTS

1 pound lentils
½ cup chopped parsley
1 red onion, chopped
1 cup chopped celery
½ pound cooked salami, cut into
   julienne strips
1 cup corn oil
⅓ cup cider vinegar
1 teaspoon salt

1 teaspoon sugar
1 tablespoon prepared mustard
Trimmed spinach leaves
4 slices crisp bacon, crumbled
Shredded carrots

Cover lentils with salted water and cook at a simmer, adding water if necessary, until lentils are tender, about 40 to 45 minutes. Drain and cool.

Add parsley, onion, celery, and salami to lentils and stir.

Beat oil with vinegar, salt, sugar, and mustard until thick. Pour dressing over salad and toss until all particles are coated. Chill.

Place salad on a nest of spinach leaves and garnish with crumbled crisp bacon and shredded carrots. Serve with slices of pumpernickel bread.

INDEX